LIGHTNING BOLT BOOKS™

The Redwood Forests

Lisa Bullard

Lerner Publications Company
Minneapolis

For Wendy,
who loves both
wild places and
good books
—L.B.

Lerner Publications Company
A division of Lerner Publishing Group, Inc.
241 First Avenue North
Minneapolis, MN 55401 U.S.A.

Website address: www.lernerbooks.com

Library of Congress Cataloging-in-Publication Data

Bullard, Lisa.
    The redwood forests / by Lisa Bullard.
        p.   cm. — (Lightning bolt books™–Famous places)
    Includes index.
    ISBN 978-0-7613-4452-0 (lib. bdg. : alk. paper)
    1. Coast redwood—Juvenile literature. I. Title.
    QK494.5.T3B85 2010
    585'.2—dc22   2009020342

Manufactured in the United States of America
1 — BP — 12/15/09

Contents

What Are the Redwood Forests?

Redwoods are very tall evergreen trees. Large groups of these trees make up the redwood forests.

Redwood forests grow only in the western United States. The forests are close to the Pacific Ocean. But they aren't too close. Redwoods don't like salty water.

Redwoods can't grow too near the ocean. Its waters are salty, and redwoods don't like salt.

The forests are mostly in northern California. But redwoods also grow in the southern part of Oregon.

A hiker walks among the California redwoods.

The Amazing Redwood

Redwoods are the tallest living things on Earth.

One redwood is more than 379 feet (115 meters) tall! That is much taller than the Statue of Liberty.

Redwoods are
not just tall.
Some are big
enough
around to drive
a car through!

A car drives through a
giant redwood in California.

Redwood bark is reddish brown or gray. The bark can be 1 foot (0.3 m) thick.

Some redwoods are reddish brown, like the one on the left. Others are gray, like the one on the right.

Redwoods grow where it is often foggy. Redwood needles take in wetness from the fog. This provides water to the treetops.

How a Redwood Grows

Cones grow on redwood trees. The cones hold and protect the trees' seeds. The seeds are only as big as tomato seeds.

Many redwoods do not grow from seeds.

Instead, they spring up
from redwood stumps.
Or they grow from fallen
branches, roots, or burls.
A burl is a kind of lump
on the tree.

New redwood trees
grow from a fallen
redwood log.

Redwoods can grow several feet in only one year.

A young redwood tree grows beside a giant.

Redwoods often grow new trunks high in the forest canopy. The canopy is made up of the highest treetops and branches in the forest.

Some redwoods have been alive for more than two thousand years. They continue to grow as long as they live.

Older redwoods can survive fires!

Sometimes a fire hollows out a cave in a redwood's trunk. But the redwood still keeps growing.

This redwood tree has a big cave in its trunk.

At Home the Forest

Redwood forests are home to many living things. Tall Douglas firs and other trees grow near redwoods.

Douglas firs share the forest with redwood trees.

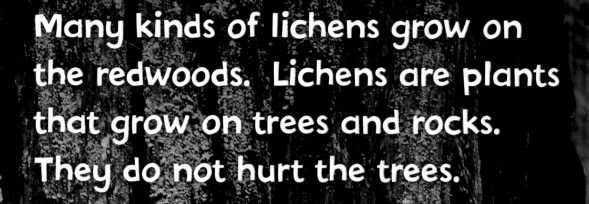

Many kinds of lichens grow on the redwoods. Lichens are plants that grow on trees and rocks. They do not hurt the trees.

Green lichen coats the trunk of this redwood.

Ferns and other plants often grow on fallen trees.

Young ferns cover this fallen redwood log.

Large animals, such as black bears, live in redwood forests.

21

Smaller animals, like banana slugs, do too.

A banana slug slides along a redwood trunk.

Northern spotted owls depend on tall trees.

Shade from the redwoods keeps forest streams cool. This cooling shade protects the fish that live there.

Berry bushes and even small trees grow high in the treetops. Animals such as salamanders live in the canopy too.

A researcher finds a salamander in the canopy of a redwood forest.

Saving the Redwood Forests

The redwood forests used to be much larger. But many of the giant trees have been cut down. People used them to build things like houses and decks.

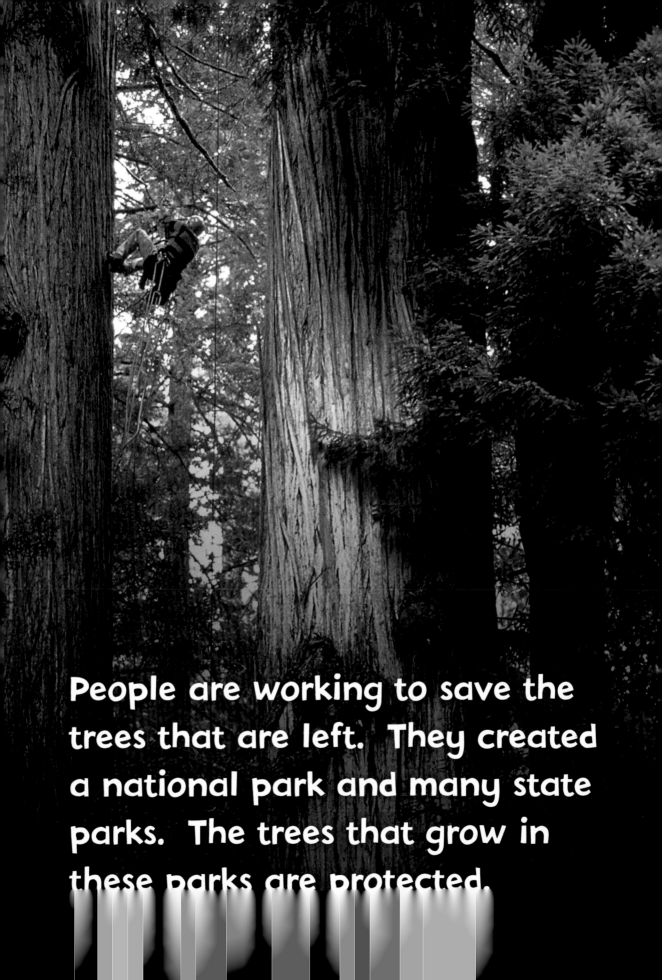

People are working to save the trees that are left. They created a national park and many state parks. The trees that grow in these parks are protected.

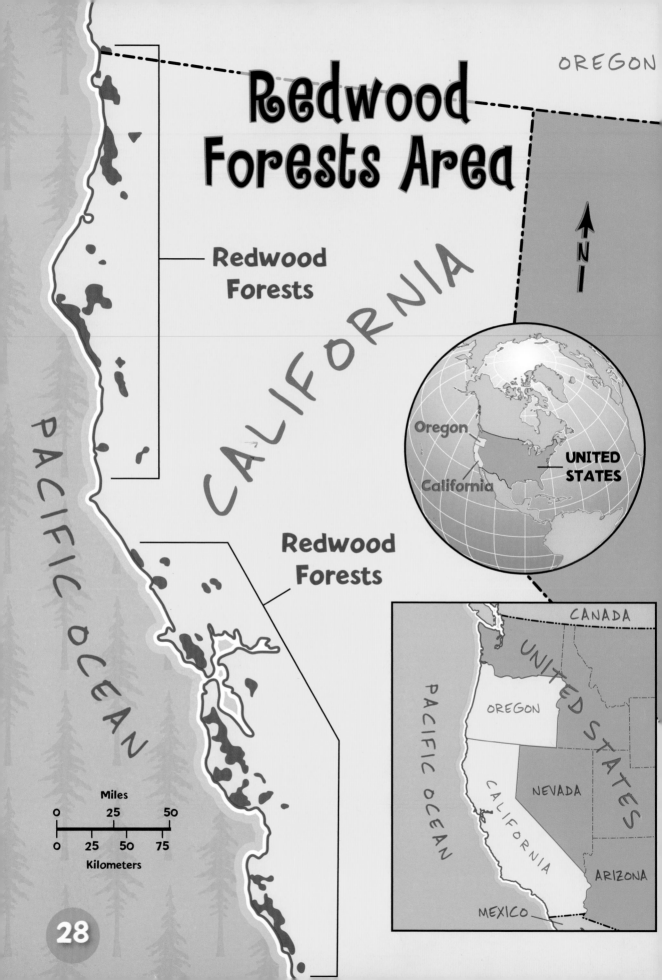

Redwood Forests Area

OREGON

Redwood
Forests

CALIFORNIA

Redwood
Forests

PACIFIC OCEAN

N

Oregon

California

UNITED
STATES

Miles
0   25   50

0   25   50   75
Kilometers

CANADA

UNITED STATES

OREGON

PACIFIC OCEAN

NEVADA

CALIFORNIA

ARIZONA

MEXICO

28

Fun Facts

- When people talk about redwoods, they usually mean the coast redwood. That is the redwood shown in this book. But two other trees are sometimes called redwoods. One is the giant sequoia in California. The other is the dawn redwood in China.

- Redwoods often survive fires and floods. And no insects can kill a redwood. But high winds can take down even the biggest trees.

- Sometimes new redwood trees grow up in a circle around an old stump. These are called fairy circles.

- Studying a forest's canopy is not easy. Some scientists use ropes to get up there. Then they can study the canopy up close. Sometimes, scientists even sleep in the treetops!

- Some of the world's other tallest trees are also found on the West Coast of the United States. These include the Douglas fir, the Sitka spruce, and the giant sequoia.

Glossary

bark: the outside covering of a tree's trunk and branches

burl: a lumpy growth on a redwood. A burl can grow into a new tree when a redwood is cut, damaged, or diseased.

canopy: a part of a forest made up of the highest treetops and branches

cone: the seedpod of an evergreen tree

evergreen: a tree that has green leaves or needles all year long

lichen: a plant that grows in patches on rocks and trees

needle: a kind of leaf that is thin and often pointed like a pin

salamander: a kind of amphibian that looks something like a lizard

Further Reading

Chin, Jason. *Redwoods*. New York: Roaring Brook Press, 2009.

Ecology of the Redwood Forest
http://www.humboldt.k12.ca.us/fortuna_un/5-8/redwood_forest/index.htm

Fleisher, Paul. *Forest Food Webs*. Minneapolis: Lerner Publications Company, 2008.

Gaff, Jackie. *I Wonder Why Pine Trees Have Needles: And Other Questions about Forests*. Boston: Kingfisher, 2005.

Gibbons, Gail. *Tell Me, Tree: All about Trees for Kids*. Boston: Little Brown and Company, 2002.

Hillman, Ben. *How Big Is It?: A Big Book All about Bigness*. New York: Scholastic Reference, 2007.

National Park Service:
Just for Kids
http://www.nps.gov/archive/redw/kids.html

Save the Redwoods League
http://www.savetheredwoods.org/education/foi.shtml

Index

Photo Acknowledgments

The images in this book are used with the permission of: © Mauritius/SuperStock, pp. 4, 19; © Carr Clifton/Minden Pictures, p. 5; © Art Wolfe/Stone/Getty Images, p. 6; © Gary Brettnacher/Photographer's Choice/Getty Images, p. 7; © Phil Schermeister/National Geographic Image Collection, p. 8; © Andy Ryan/The Image Bank/Getty Images, p. 9; © Miguel Salmeron/The Image Bank/Getty Images, p. 10; © Ron Crabtree/Digital Vision/Getty Images, p. 11; © Ed Reschke/Peter Arnold, Inc., p. 12; © Fabian Gonzales Editorial/Alamy, p. 13; © Flirt/SuperStock, p. 14; © Philip Nealey/Photodisc/Getty Images, p. 15; © Steve Satushek/Riser/Getty Images, p. 16; © Dennis Frates/Alamy, p. 17; © Martin Page/Photolibrary/Getty Images, p. 18; © Jack Dykinga/Riser/Getty Images, p. 20; © Dave King/Dorling Kindersley/Getty Images, p. 21; © Roy Toft/Photolibrary/Getty Images, p. 22; © Greg Vaughn/Stone/Getty Images, p. 23; © Philip Hutson/Alamy, p. 24; © Peter Lane Taylor/Visuals Unlimited, Inc., pp. 25, 27; © Mark E. Gibson/CORBIS, p. 26; © Laura Westlund/Independent Picture Service, p. 28; © Gerald and Buff Corsi/Visuals Unlimited, Inc., p. 30; © Michael Sewell/Peter Arnold, Inc., p. 31.

Front Cover: © Dennis Frates/Alamy